SELF-REALIZATION

FROM BHAGWADGITA

KRISHNA MURARI SONI

Contents

Preface

Arjun was a great leader, good listener, knowledgeable but an emotional person. There is nothing wrong to be emotional but emotions should be shown according to the situation. Emotions should also not overpower wisdom.

During Kurukshetra war, Arjun's emotions overpowered his wisdom. So much so that he asked Lord Krishna the purpose of fighting Kurukshetra war. Then Lord Krishna told him the importance of *karma* i.e. performing action. This dialogue between Arjun and Lord Krishna is compiled in Bhagwadgita. After listening to Lord Krishna, Arjun decided to fight the battle.

Though Bhagwadgita is said to be a proceeding of the dialogue in the battlefield between Lord Krishna and Arjun, it is not the story of Kurukshetra war. It describes various paths to reach the state of self-realization however it is not possible without performing action (*karma*).

I thought to write about self-realization as described in Bhagwadgita with my very limited understanding. As such, it is not exact version or with exact interpretation but in simplified form for the persons like me who are not the experts. Those, who want to go into deeper understanding, can always refer Bhagwadgita written by the learned scholars.

(Krishna Murari Soni)

CHAPTER ONE

About the Characters of Bhagwadgita

1. Abhimanyu was son of Arjun and Subhadra.
2. Arjun was third Pandav, son of Kunti, a great archer and close friend of Krishna, married to Subhadra.
3. Ashwatthama was son of guru Dronacharya.
4. Bhim was second Pandav, younger to Yudhishthir and elder to Arjun.
5. Bhishm, also known as Gangaputra, was eldest son of king Shantanu of Hastinapur, and Ganga. King Shantanu layer married to Satyavati whose father asked king Shantanu to declare son of Satyavati as successor after him. Bhishm vowed not to marry forever and as such gave way for the marriage of Satyavati to king Shantanu. Vichitravirya was the son of king Shantanu and Satyavati hence step brother of Bhishm. Thus, Bhishm was grandfather of Pandav and Kaurav who called him *Pitamah*. He was a great warrior and remained attached forever to the throne of Hastinapur.
6. Bhurishrawa was grandson of king Bahalika, brother of Shantanu.
7. Cekitana was the son of king Dhristketu and king of Kaikaya.
8. Dhritrashtra was elder son of Vichitravirya, king of Hastinapur. He was blind by birth, due to which his younger brother Pandu was made king of Hastinapur. However, after immature death of Pandu Dhritrashtra was made the king of Hastinapur.
9. Dhristketu was the king of Chedi and army general of Pandav's army during Mahabharat.
10. Draupadi was daughter of Drupad and wife of Pandav.
11. Dronacharya was the guru (teacher) of Pandav and Kaurav. He was the childhood friend of king Drupad who insulted him after becoming the king. He had one son by name Ashwatthama.

12. Drupad was the king of Panchal. Dhristdumn, Draupadi and Shikhandi (born as girl Shikhandini) were his children.

13. Duryodhan was the eldest son of Dhritrashtra and his wife Gandhari. Dhritrashtra and Gandhari had one hundred sons and a daughter named Dushala who was married to Jaydrath.

14. Gandeev was the name of the bow of Arjun.

15. Hastinapur is a place near Meerut city in Uttar Pradesh state of India.

16. Janak was father of Sita.

17. Jaydrath was the king of Sindhu and brother in law of Duryodhan, married to Dushala, only sister of one hundred Kaurav.

18. Karn was the eldest son of Kunti. She left him after giving birth to him before marriage. He was brought up by Adhirath (a charioteer) and his wife Radha. He was a great warrior. Duryodhan befriended him seeing his strength and valour.

19. Kripacharya was also the guru (teacher) of Pandav and Kaurav and a council member of Kuru kingdom.

20. Krishna was the son of Vasudev and Devaki, brought up by Nand and Yashoda and an incarnation of Lord Vishnu.

21. Kuntibhoj was father of Kunti.

22. Kuru was a legendary king in India whose descendants were known as Kaurav. To differentiate two sides of a family of king Dhritrashtra and Pandu, the sons of Dhritrashtra are known as Kaurav and of Pandu as Pandav.

23. Kurukshetra is the place where Mahabharat was fought. At present, it is in Haryana state of India.

24. Mahabharat is a great war fought between Pandav and Kaurav in Kurukshetra in which almost all the kings and warriors of that period participated.

25. Pandav were sons of king Pandu. Pandu was made king of Hastinapur as his elder brother Dhritrashtra was blind. He had two wives as Kunti and Madri. Kunti had four sons i.e. Karn, Yudhishthir, Bhim, and Arjun while Madri two as Nakul and Sahdev. Kunti left Karn immediately after the birth. Pandu's sons Yudhishthir, Bhim, Arjun, Nakul and Sahdev were called Pandav.

26. Pandu was son of Vichitravirya and younger brother of Dhritrashtra.

27. Purujit was son of king Kuntibhoj and brother of Kunti, mother of Pandav.

28. Sanjay was the advisor of king Dhritrashtra who narrated Mahabharat war live to Dhritrashtra.

29. Satyaki was a Yadav chieftain and fought from the side of Pandav.

30. Saibya was the king of Suvira, a great archer, whose daughter was married to Akrur, a chieftain of Yadav's army.

31. Subhadra was the daughter of Vasudev and Rohini.

32. Vasudev was Lord Krishna's father.

33. Vikarn was a brother of Duryodhan.

34. Virat was the king of Matsya kingdom and father in law of Abhimanyu, son of Arjun and Subhadra.

35. Yudhumanyu and Uttamaujas were brothers of Draupadi.

CHAPTER TWO

Arjun's Grief

Dhritrashtra asked Sanjay about the happenings at the battlefield of Kurukshetra where his sons and Pandav had assembled. Sanjay told him that Duryodhan after looking at the army of Pandav spoke to Dronacharya to behold the Pandav's army led by Dhristdumn having warriors such as Satyaki, Virat and Drupad, nobles such as Dhrastketu, Cekitana, Purujit, Kuntibhoj and Saibya, and valiant such as Yudhumanyu, Uttamauja, Abhimanyu, and sons of Draupadi. Then Duryodhan told Dronacharya about warriors of his side having him (Dronacharya), Bhishm, Karn, Kripacharya, Ashwatthama, Vikarn, Bhurisrawa and Jaydrath equipped with great weapons, protected by Bhishm having unlimited strength compared to the Pandav's army protected by Bhim and then asked everyone to protect Bhishm from all the strategic points.

After the briefing by Duryodhan, Bhishm blew his conch shell to mark the commencement of battle from Kaurav's side followed by roaring sound of conch shells, trumpets, kettledrums etc. by their army. In reply, Lord Krishna and Arjun also blew their conch shells followed by the others of Pandav's army to show their strength to Kaurav.

Then Arjun requested Lord Krishna to place his chariot between both the armies so that he could have a look on those he is required to fight and were well-wishers of Duryodhan.

Lord Krishna then placed the chariot between both the armies in front of Bhishm, Dronacharya and other kings assembled there, from where Arjun was able to see those with whom he was to fight including his elders, guru (teachers), maternal uncles, brothers, sons, grandsons, friends, father in laws etc. Seeing his kinsmen assembled to fight, Arjun said to Lord Krishna that his mouth is drying up, limbs weakening, body trembling, skin burning and Gandeev slipping from his hands, mind becoming unsteady, not desiring victory, kingdom or joy of winning. He told that he did not see any good in slaying his own kinsmen even for the victory of kingdom of the three worlds.

Many a times two leaders make the arguments due to superiority complex between the two. Lord Krishna was regarded as a great leader by most of the kings of that period, even by Bhishm, Dronacharya, Yudhishthir and Duryodhan. He knew that Arjun will become emotional once he saw his Pitamah (Bhishm), Guru (Dronacharya) and other kin assembled there to fight. Still, he obeyed Arjun and placed the chariot between the two armies. Thus, he did not get engaged in the argument. It gives us a learning that a problem can be solved in a better way by avoiding argument. Also, a self-realized person is always calm in favourable or adverse situations.

Elders are always to be respected and one should not quarrel or fight with them. But, in the battlefield even relatives are to be treated as enemy if fighting from opposite side as performing duty is to be given superiority.

He further told to Lord Krishna that even though those assembled to fight with him are greedy and doing sinful action, Pandav should refrain from such action understanding the grievous crime which would be committed from the war as destruction of family members leads to the destruction of spiritual traditions forever, degradation of woman values, and a hellish situation to both the families thus it would be better to get slain remaining unarmed from the sons of Dhritrashtra.

Arjun was a great thinker and had fore sightedness. He could very well foresee the outcome of the war. Even today, one has to realize outcome of a war hence should go for it only after careful consideration of its outcome as Arjun mentioned. The war not only leads to the destruction of wealth but also of values and traditions. Women are most affected due to war in terms of values and tradition. They lead hellish situations so also their children. Therefore, a leader whether in winning or losing position, has to realize such situation before taking any decision.

Thereafter, Arjun kept his Gandeev aside.

CHAPTER THREE

Knowledge

Arjun was not ready to attack or counterattack his *pitamah* (grandfather) Bhishm and guru Dronacharya to win and get back the kingdom. He was even of the view that after slaying their cousins, Pandav may not have any desire to live even if they win. Therefore, he told Lord Krishna that weakness was overpowering his wisdom and thoughts resulting into indecisiveness regarding right path to be followed as his senses were getting filled with grief and unable to think.

Emotional weakness can overpower strength, courage, bravery, and mind hence the performance. A true leader always controls his weakness so also the emotions. Emotional weakness can result into disaster during a war.

Lord Krishna told Arjun that your emotional weakness is overpowering your worth before the enemy. You are knowledgeable and a knowledgeable person neither feels grief nor laments for a dead or living person. I, you and all these kings assembled here to fight were existing at all the time and will exist in future also. Just as the body changes from childhood to youth to old age, soul also migrates from one body to another. Soul is always live and body is not soul. Soul does not have grief or pleasure. Body senses feel cold, heat, pleasure, and pain which are temporary in nature.

A self-realized person does not show weakness as it overpowers wisdom. To remove emotional weakness, Lord Krishna told Arjun that everyone is always live.

As per the Bhagwadgita, every living body always existed and will always exist like energy. It provides the concept of rebirth though rebirth may be in human or non-human form. Thus, birth and death are the stages of a body and not of soul. Soul is indestructible, everlasting, immortal and imperishable.

If one is alive, no one feels grieved and if body is dead, it immediately takes birth. Thus, a soul is always live and one should not feel grieved for the live. When body becomes old, no one feels grieved and if death is also another stage, one should not feel grieved for another stage of life.

It means that one should never feel grieved even under adverse conditions. When even death and birth are the stages of life, grieves and happiness should not be linked to them. Thus, Lord Krishna says that one should not feel grief in the life.

And you should know, soul in the body is imperishable and indestructible and without soul, body is dead. No one can destruct soul. Soul neither slays anyone nor can slay anyone. Soul never takes birth nor dies at any time as soul is immortal, everlasting, imperishable and timeless. Though soul is the source of life, it never dies on destruction of the body. Being unborn, indestructible, un-deteriorating and everlasting, no one can cause death to soul even if someone slays to a person. Soul accepts new body just as a person gives up old or worn out clothes and accepts new ones. Weapons cannot harm soul, fire cannot burn soul, water cannot wet soul and air cannot dry up soul. Soul is invisible, inconceivable, and immutable. Therefore, one should not mourn for it.

A self-realized person understands that soul is like energy which never gets destructed and changes the form only. Since soul is indestructible, it cannot be slayed. So body is slayed or dies, not the soul.

There are numerous material desires and these are only for the body which is destructible by sure. One has to decide whether to perform action for the body only or for the body and soul.

And if you think soul is always live, you should not mourn as it immediately accepts new body once it has left old. One who has taken birth, death is certain and for the one who is dead, birth is certain and thus birth and death are inevitable events as such you should not mourn on death.

Lord Krishna says that birth and death are inevitable events and thus one has to take them as usual events. One has to realize that even mourning on death is not a permanent and has to perform action even after death of the body of a near and dear one. If one realizes that he or she is to be away from grieves under all situations, moves towards the state of self-realization.

Arjun, human beings know only the events between birth and death but not those before the birth or after the death. Therefore, there is no ground to mourn for the unknowns.

We, human beings cannot foresee the future so also do not know about the previous birth(s). And it is really helpful in minimizing the grieves. If one could have known events of previous birth(s) or was able to know the future, situation might have been miserable both due to past of earlier life and of the future.

Some consider soul as amazing, some describe as amazing, some hear soul to be amazing and some even do not have any knowledge of soul even if having heard about it. Arjun, soul is everlasting and immortal within every living body so for immortal, why to mourn? Moreover, you have to perform your *karma* (duty/action), fighting the battle. If you do not perform your duty, you will lose your reputation and incur a sinful action resulting into people speaking about your infamy forever, a situation worse than death for a respected and reputed person as warriors standing opposite to you will consider you coward, leaving battle out of fear. Such a situation will also be disgraceful to those you carry high esteem. Your enemies will speak many insulting words regarding you which will be very painful. Getting slain with performing virtuous action by way of fighting the battle will result into attainment of heaven and getting win into the enjoyment of the Earth. Therefore, be confident and fight.

One is remembered for his or her actions. Reputation is directly linked to one's performance of the action or duty one is supposed to do. If one does not perform required duty, it leads to infamy which maybe for many generations. Enemies, common people and even close relatives may humiliate and insult such a person so much so that getting slain by fighting becomes a better option. Therefore, everyone should realize that one should not shirk his or her responsibility of performing dutiful action.

When one shirks responsibility or does not perform his or her duty due to any reason, others consider it is due to fear. Leaving the field of duty due to fear is considered cowardice in every field of work.

If you have equanimity to pleasure and grief, advantage and disadvantage, victory and defeat, you will do no sinful reaction therefore fight the battle without thinking of result.

It is important to perform the dutiful action without looking towards its result and the result has to be accepted as it is. This leads to the path of self-realization.

We perform other than virtuous action either for pleasure or grief for ourselves or others. If one is able to have equanimity to pleasure and grief, will perform only virtuous action and remain happy. Pleasure and happiness are different as pleasure is for short term while happiness is permanent. Knowledge of attaining happiness leads to the path of self-realization.

Lord Krishna then told that performing virtuous action is extremely important as even slight virtuous action saves from a greater danger. Ultimate knowledge deals with the knowledge of temperaments, knowledge of self-realization, knowledge of getting free from duality, and knowledge of getting free from materialistic possessions.

Performing dutiful virtuous action leads to happiness and saves from grieves. Performing virtuous action leads to self-realization.

And you certainly have the right to perform action but have no right on its result hence your motivation should not be attached to the result of performing action or not to perform virtuous action. As such, perform your virtuous action giving up attachment to its result and keeping equanimity during success and failure both. Keeping equanimity during success and failure is a part of the Ultimate knowledge so perform your action giving up desire or attachment to the result of action.

One has the right to decide whether to perform virtuous action or no action or forbidden action but has no right of its outcome. We, even in our daily life, perform action with the desire of its outcome or result on which have no right. When the result is not favourable, we feel grieved and when favourable feel pleasure for a short term even if the success was not due to us as it is not in our control and thus taking its credit may offend others. Therefore, if one wants to be away from the grieves and also want to keep them away from others, should perform action without desire of attachment to its result. Once it is followed, one moves towards self-realization.

On getting the Ultimate knowledge, one gets rid of positive or negative reactions of one's action. Hence try to follow the path of getting Ultimate knowledge as persons having its knowledge liberate themselves from the result of their actions and attain self-realization. Once you achieve such a state, you will have equanimity and remain unaffected and uninfluenced of actions and reactions, thus attaining the Ultimate knowledge.

Every action has its reaction. If one performs virtuous action, its reaction would also be virtuous though not in the hands of the doer. Thus, for every action there may be positive or negative reaction. Lord Krishna says to Arjun to have the Ultimate knowledge that reaction is not in your control as such you have to perform action without desire of its positive reaction.

One should perform action without desire of its result and consider the result of positive or negative reaction with equanimity. Once, one has this knowledge and is able to implement in oneself, gets the knowledge and then moves towards attaining the state of self-realization. Once self-realized, one gets rid of action and reaction as a self-realized person always does virtuous action treating all the reactions with equanimity.

Arjun asked Lord Krishna about the indicators of attaining Ultimate knowledge. Lord Krishna said when one gives up all desires for gratification of senses including from the mind, attains the Ultimate knowledge. Then his mind is undisturbed by stress, desires, attachment, fear and anger. Such a person is neither grieved nor has pleasure due to withdrawal from the gratification of senses and remains happy without depending on the material desires.

Desire of sense gratification disturbs the mind. Undisturbed mind results into stress, desires, attachments, fear and anger. When one performs action without material desires, withdraws from their gratification and as such remains happy under all situations. Thus, a person without stress, attachment, fear, anger but having controlled mind is knowledgeable.

Krishna told Arjun that even a person with awakened mind can surrender to senses gratification hence one should do meditation and bring senses under control. A person while concentrating on the objectives of the senses develops attachment to the senses from which material desires are born and from non-gratification or partial gratification of desires anger arises. From anger, obsession occurs, from obsession mind disturbance leading to loss of wisdom but a person controlling self is able to control senses, keeping free from obsession remaining away from evils and happy attaining peace.

Knowledgeable knows that anger and fear arise due to partial or non-gratification of senses leading to disturbance of mind and loss of wisdom thus brings senses under control. Once able to bring senses under control, moves towards attaining self-realization.

Sage achieves peace being unaffected by desires of sense gratifications due to giving up all material desires remaining away from attachments, ego and possessions.

One unaffected from the desire of sense gratifications attains peace.

CHAPTER FOUR

Karma-Performing Action

Lord Krishna told that there are two paths to attain self-realization in this world, one the path of knowledge for knowledge seekers and the other, path of action (*karma*) for yogis. Self-realization can neither be achieved without performing action (*karma*) nor by renouncing action (*karma*) altogether. Living bodies always perform some action as they cannot remain without performing action even for a moment.

For gaining self-realization, there are different paths. One of the paths is gaining knowledge. Once, one gains knowledge, starts moving on the prescribed path of self-realization. Another path is performing required action but virtuous. Even for gaining knowledge, one has to perform action. Thus, performing action is essential in all the paths.

Self-realization is a state which can be achieved only through a process. This process involves specific stages. Also, self-realization is not a normal state hence everyone cannot achieve it as it is not feasible for everyone to renounce material desires and attachments altogether. However, one can move towards attaining self-realization by controlling the material desires and attachments.

Self-realization cannot not be achieved without performing action and such an action has to be virtuous, performed by controlling desires and mind.

Those controlling five working sense organs but thinking about the sense objectives in their mind are hypocrites. One, controlling the senses from the mind and performing virtuous action without attachment to the desire of its result is superior and knowledgeable.

Lord Krishna says that control of sense organs is not enough but mind has also to be controlled. Many a times, one controls the senses due to fear, or greed i.e. personal gains. These senses go out of control when situation changes. Sometimes, one is not able to control senses in the mind. One has to control sense organs through body and mind. Once, one reaches to such a state, approaches towards self-realization. One controlling senses from the body but not from the mind is hypocrite and cannot move towards self-realization.

Perform your virtuous action since performing action is better than renouncing action as without action even body survival is not possible. Arjun, everyone is bound by the action performed except one renounced to God, being free from the desire of its result. One should adopt renunciation as it pleases even to deities and as such first offer your action to God. Various activities in the universe are driven through sacrifice or offering to others. Persons devotedly offering even small food items, flowers and petals to God relieve themselves from the sins.

One has to perform action even for the survival. This action should be virtuous. When one offers action to God, gets rid of its reaction.

When one offers his or her action to God, performs only virtuous action as a devotee cannot offer something to God which is not virtuous and thus always performs godly action. Lord Krishna says that one is relieved of the sins even by offering small items like food, flowers and petals. Thus, one offering action also gets relieved from its reaction. When one devotedly offers every action to Him thus performing only godly action from body and mind, reaches to the state of self-realization.

Life is based on food, food is produced from rainfall, rainfall occurs from the offerings and sense of offerings originates from performing virtuous action. Thus, all offerings or sacrifices originate from performing action. Therefore, perform your virtuous action without any desire of its result. By performing virtuous action, king Janak and many others reached the state of self-realization likewise you should also perform your virtuous action for the welfare of people as common man follows to great personalities. For God, there is no prescribed action in any world, still He is engaged in the action. If god renounces the action, certainly all humans would follow the same path and living entities would get ruined and destroyed.

Nothing comes without performing action or karma. Even God performs action as the creator, sustainer and destroyer. Hence, one should never renounce action. As God is never attached to His action or its result, one should not get attached to the action or its result rather perform it as the duty. As He performs His action for the welfare of the universe, one should also perform action for the welfare of the universe. When one is able to do it, moves towards the state of self-realization.

As ignorant perform action with the desire to its result, knowledgeable should perform action for the welfare of the world. All the actions are influenced by the senses in the material world and ignorant get attached to them thinking themselves as the performers of the actions. But a knowledgeable knows about the doer and performs virtuous action without desire of the result of the action.

All actions are influenced by the senses hence it is common to get attached to them but a knowledgeable by doing virtuous action for the welfare of the universe moves towards the state of self-realization.

Those offering all actions to God, seeking knowledge of self, having no attachment to material desires, free from accumulations & possessions and pain arising from it, and having faith in God without envy to others become free from bondage of the reaction of their actions. But those being envy to others do not have knowledgeable or ignore knowledge being deviated from the purpose of welfare of the universe. All actions are performed as per the nature and temperaments and even knowledgeable perform actions as per their temperaments. Attraction and attachment to the senses though are part of the management, one should not be controlled by the senses. Lord Krishna said that performing own duty even with faults is better than performing other's duty perfectly as it is fraught with danger.

Pain and grief arise due to attachment to material desires leading to the desires of accumulation and possessions of the objects. These are due to desires related to self viz self-body and mind, self-family and friends, self-needs and possessions, and self-ego. When one is able to think and perform action beyond self, reaches to self-realization state.

Lord Krishna says that performing own action without perfection is better than performing other's action perfectly i.e. one has to first perform own action perfectly and if not able to do so even without perfection. When one is able to perform own action perfectly, then only should venture into other's work.

Arjun asked what incites one to perform sinful action even against one's own will.

Lord Krishna said, it is the lust or desire arising out of extravagance. Lust or desire is the greatest enemy to oneself being insatiable and extremely sinful as it covers the wisdom even of a knowledgeable person engaged in controlling senses and mind. Therefore, Arjun, you should bring senses under control first and destroy lust, cause of sins, destroyer of knowledge and realization. And senses are controlled by mind and mind is controlled by intelligence and intelligence is controlled by knowledge.

Lord Krishna says that lust or desire in the mind forces one to perform action other than the virtuous. Such action is performed to gratify the lust or material desires arising out of extravagance or greed. In case, one is not able to control them, sense gratification controls mind and mind overpowers the knowledge and wisdom. Thus, one has to control senses and mind. When one is able to do so, moves towards self-realization.

CHAPTER FIVE

Wisdom

Lord Krishna told Arjun that I am aware of my births and also of yours but not you. Although birthless, immortal and immutable, I appear and reappear whenever and wherever *dharm* (Divine activities) declines and rise of *adharm* (demonic activities) is predominant to protect devotees of *dharma* and eradication of those involved in sinful activities.

There is a supreme power aware of everything including pre-birth histories of all living entities though they are not aware of it. Such supreme power appears and reappears from time to time to save the destruction.

Those free from the material desires, having no fear or anger, devoted to Me, knowledgeable, submitting to Me are rewarded by Me as they follow the path of virtuous action. However, those having unsatisfied material desires worship deities (said to be god of those material desires). Although all human beings are created by Me based on their nature, temperaments and performed actions, I am not attached to them. Actually, attachment to performing action is neither for Me nor the desire of the result of My action is for Me. One who understands it and follows Me, never gets attached to the desire and result of the performing action.

Humans worship or follow to various deities, or the supreme power. Those devoted to the supreme power, are free from the material desires due to performing virtuous action. Those devoted to other deities for fulfilling the material desires are involved in them hence not able to achieve the state of self-realization.

One has to understand action (*karma*), forbidden action (*vikarma*) and inaction (*akarma*). One who looks inaction in performing (virtuous) action (performing action so effortlessly that looks like no action being performed such as breathing), and performs (virtuous) action during inaction (mentally performing action during inactive stage) is a perfect performer of action. One becomes perfect performer of all the actions when performing every action without any desire or attachment to its result. A person having no material desire having able to control body and mind, and beyond the state of possessions always remains contended with whatever comes on own accord and is tolerant to dualities (favourable and unfavourable conditions), having equanimity during success and failure and no jealousy. A *karmyogi* (action performer) offers his or her actions, *gyanyogi* (knowledgeable) makes sacrifice delivering knowledge, a renunciate (*sanyasi*) sacrifices sense gratification and others exercise self-control of senses through meditation for attaining wisdom of self-realization. Some are engaged in charity donating their possessions, performing austerities and penance as sacrifice and some are making sacrifices in acquiring knowledge. Some control breath cycle and some food intake to make sacrifices. All these sacrifices are made to attain wisdom.

Every human being performs action (karma) however karma maybe vikarma i.e. forbidden action, or satkarma i.e. virtuous action however there is also a state of akarma (inaction). When karma is performed like akarma, it does not require effort and as such one does not get tired or feel stressed. For example, one doing daily exercise as a routine not feeling stress reaches to the state of akarma however one doing occasional exercise will feel tired. Therefore, karma has to be satkarma (virtuous) and to be performed so devotedly that it becomes akarma (inaction). Performing virtuous action like inaction leads to self-realization path.

On attaining the state of self-realization, one performs every action without any desire and desire of attachment to its result. This is possible only when one is able to perform action without any material desire with controlled mind and body. Such a person is always contended, has equanimity between favourable and unfavourable conditions, and has no jealousy to anyone. Such a condition is achieved by virtuous action performer (karmyogi), knowledge seeker (gyanyogi), or renunciate (sanyasi). A karmyogi does not have any material desire and is unattached to the result of the action by the performed action, gyanyogi has knowledge of the path of self-realization and moves on it and a sanyasi renounces the desires and attachments hence all three paths lead to the state of self-realization. To control mind and body, various activities are taken including meditation, yoga, austerities, penance, charity, and knowledge gaining from the knowledgeable.

Arjun, everyone has to sacrifice for being fit to remain in this universe and offering (sacrifice) knowledge is better than sacrifice of material possessions.

CHAPTER SIX

Renunciation

Lord Krishna told that renunciation and performing virtuous action both lead to the path of attaining moksha (liberation from cycle of birth and death) however performing virtuous action is superior. The one who renounces desire of the result of action is always a renunciate and is free from the dualities. One having renounced action or virtuous action is not knowledgeable. Knowledgeable is one who performs action and virtuous action to gain results of the both.

Paths of renunciation and performing virtuous action both lead to self-realization even though performing virtuous action is superior. During renunciation, one generally goes to a secluded place, performs meditation and yoga for giving up material desires and desire of gratification due to limited or no material available to gratify the desires. In the path of performing virtuous action, one controls mind and material desires and thus even remaining in the material world, does not get attached to them therefore is a true renunciate having control over mind and material desires which is superior to the renunciation (sanyas).

The renunciation is also achieved by performing virtuous action. Renunciation without performing action leads to misery. Performing virtuous action with controlled mind and senses without getting attached into them helps in attaining self-realization. After self-realization, one performs action effortlessly thus reaching stage of inaction (*akarma*) in spite of seeing, hearing, touching, smelling, eating, moving, sleeping, breathing, speaking, excreting and grasping and never thinks he is performing action like opening and closing of eye lids. One who performs action dedicating to God even after living in the world of attachments, is not involved in sinful action. Performing virtuous action with controlled body and mind, and having knowledge of controlling senses for purifying self gets continual peace and happiness.

Though renunciation is related to renouncing desires, it also requires performing action or karma as renunciation without performing action (karma) leads to addiction, inadvertency, and laziness thus to misery. With such a state, one can never reach to the state of self-realization.

Therefore, both the paths require performing virtuous action as such performing virtuous action is the pre-condition of attainment of state of self-realization. Also, for performing virtuous action through body and mind, one has to control body senses and mind. Such a state can only be achieved by practicing performing virtuous action with controlling body and mind or offering all actions to God devotedly as one cannot offer anything to God which is not virtuous.

One, who renounces desires from the mind and body, does not think oneself as the doer of the action and remain happy as per the temperament. Though sins and virtues remain with the performer of the action but the knowledge destroys the ignorance. Those considering all living entities with equanimity, meditating in inner self, considering pleasure and grief with equanimity, free from dualities, win the hearts of all in the world and attain *moksha*, neither rejoicing nor lamenting during favourable and unfavourable conditions. One whose mind is not attached to senses enjoys the happiness of inner self.

On renouncing desires from the body and mind, one considers Him as the doer of the activities hence remains happy. Though sins and virtues remain with the performer of the action, being attached to it, knowledge destroys ignorance due to which one tends to be away from sinful action. Thus, knowledge is important for self-realization. A knowledgeable person considers all living entities with equanimity, listens to inner energy or soul, and works for the welfare of the universe and moves on the path of self-realization.

Arjun, momentary pleasures arising from the sense gratification are indeed the source of misery, having a beginning and short end. A self-controlled person able to control physical, mental and emotional urges produced from the material desires and attachments, remains happy.

One who experiences internal happiness, able to see self within as well, having reached to self-realization stage, working for the welfare of all living bodies, free from lust, fear and anger, having controlled the mind, desires and senses, performing meditation certainly achieves the Ultimate truth.

A self-realized person knows about the happiness and source of misery, grieves and pains. The happiness is achieved by performing action for the welfare of the universe, which is possible when one is free from lust, fear and anger, has controlled mind, desires, senses of body and mind through meditation.

With internal happiness, one is able to understand self and attains self-realization and peace.

CHAPTER SEVEN

Meditation

Lord Krishna told that a renunciate is the one who performs action without desire of its result, not the one who renounces only bodily activities. It has to be understood that without renouncing desire of the result of performed action, one cannot achieve self-realization. Thus, to attain self-realization, performing action is the means and the one who has achieved self-realization, performing action by renouncing action (inaction in action) is the means.

Renunciate is not the one who has renounced some bodily activities or sense gratifications rather is the one who renounces sense gratifications from the body and mind and performs action. Thus, a renunciate has to perform action effortlessly by renouncing material desires for attaining self-realization. A self-realized person has to perform all actions effortlessly without any desire.

One attains self-realization when able to renounce material desires, desire of sense gratification and desire of result of performed action by the body and mind forever as mind is the best friend for those who controls it and worst enemy for those having uncontrolled mind. On conquering the mind one has equanimity during pleasure and grief, cold and heat, honour and dishonour i.e. in all situations thus attains self-realization for whom gold and stone have equal weightage. However, superior to such a person is one having equanimity by action and thoughts to his well-wishers, enemies, envious, sinful, saints and is beyond disputes, or mediation to disputes.

Mind is the best friend if controlled and worst enemy if uncontrolled. For attaining self-realization one has to understand it and control the mind. Traits of a self-realized person are performing virtuous action, equanimity, non-envy to everyone whether friend or enemy, saint or sinful person and having no disputes with anyone of anything.

To attain such a state, one practices on self, keeping control on mind and material desires, keeping away from accumulation, engaging in inner meditation and concentration sitting on comfortable seat made of natural materials, keeping body stable with controlled and un-agitated peaceful mind, taking only as much as required for the body needs, not more not less, even food and sleep thus controlling and self-regulating body and mind without attachment to the material desires. Attaining self-realization stage, one never deviates from truth and remains happy. Such stage leads to controlled and tranquil mind without reaction, free from ego providing feeling of self in all living entities and all living entities in self and thus one sees God everywhere and in everything all the time and tries to perform virtuous action under all the circumstances, achieving equanimity.

To attain the state of self-realization, one has to practice control on self thus control on mind and material desires, control on accumulation and possessions keeping as much as required, taking as much as required even food and sleep, free from ego and seeing God in everything and everyone.

Similar is the concept of self. No one harms to self and tries to perform action for self. In case, one is able to see and feel self in all living bodies and in everything, always performs action for the welfare of the universe.

Uncontrolled mind is difficult to control being flickering, turbulent, obstinate and strong. If one is engaged in controlling the mind but has not achieved it perfectly, remains away from evils, takes birth in pious and prosperous families and regain temperaments of the previous life, thus continue gaining knowledge for many lifetimes to attain ultimate knowledge.

It is not easy to control mind. Uncontrolled mind is even more difficult to control. Therefore, it becomes difficult to attain self-realization state. One should not worry for not being able to achieve self-realization as even one's engagement in controlling the mind keeps away from the evils and one continues to gain control over the mind during the present life or other lives to come thus helping in attaining self-realization.

CHAPTER EIGHT

Ultimate Truth

Lord Krishna told that out of many thousands, one endeavors for knowing Ultimate truth and of those many endeavour, hardly one achieves it and out of those achieving, hardly one knows Me. There are eight divisions of My external energy as earth, water, air, fire, ether, mind, intelligence and ego. This external energy is inferior to inner energy embodied in the souls of living bodies by which they exist in the material world. Everything is manifested, created, sustained and destroyed in the universe by these two energies. There is nothing superior to inner energy and everything is connected through it like pearls by a thread. This energy provides taste in water, radiation in the sun and moon, tides in oceans, sound in ether, strength in humans, fertility in soil, heat in fire, and vitality in human beings to perform action. Thus, energy is contained in origin of all the living bodies, providing wisdom for knowledge and prowess for power. Even *Satgun* (verity), *Rajogun* (extravagance) and *Tamogun* (vileness) temperaments are from this energy but they are not in the energy. Complete universe gets deluded from the external energy, but no one knows Me (Inner energy), superior to external energy, supreme and indestructible. Those embracing inner energy get away from the illusion of the three temperaments of external energy though for others it is difficult to come out of them. Without knowledge of inner energy, ignorant get engaged into illusion of the material world.

It is not easy to know God or even to reach the state of self-realization. The external energy existing in the material world distracts one through earth, water, air, fire, ether, mind, intelligence and ego from the inner energy. Even though knowledgeable know about both of them and knowing fully that inner energy is superior to external energy, they may also get distracted from the inner energy due to illusion of the material world like ignorant. Temperaments are also from inner energy but they are not in it hence temperaments also get deluded from external energy.

Whole universe gets deluded from the external energy and as such very few endeavours for self-realization and out of those hardly few achieves it.

Arjun, four types of persons render devotion of seeking self-realization i.e. distressed, knowledge seekers, desirous of wealth, and wise. Among those wise are superior and close to achieve it.

Distressed, knowledge seekers, desirous of wealth and wise persons think to move on the path of self-realization but only wise are able to move on it and others leave it.

After innumerable births, rare one gains knowledge to understand Me. Those having various desires worship deities to fulfill desires due to ignorance and inadequate knowledge. Their desires get fulfilled as per their efforts and faith in the worship.

Mostly people get distracted from the path of self-realization and few even after gaining inadequate knowledge worship to those whom they consider are able to fulfil their desires and may even get them fulfilled from the deities they worship. But only rare gains self-realization after innumerable births. Thus, one should continue to gain the knowledge and move on the path of self-realization as it does not get waste.

Arjun, I know the past, present and future of all living entities but no one knows Me. All living entities get illusion by duality of energy resulting into desires, malice and outrunning others but those seeking knowledge and getting wise about Me, are free from the duality of illusion and are liberated from weakness and fear of death, knowing self, action and reaction. With the knowledge of Ultimate truth, they understand Me with their minds absorbed in Me even at the moment of the death.

Though God knows past, present and future of all living bodies, living bodies are unaware of their previous birth(s) and future. Further, they have illusion of external energy, impact of action and reaction and fear of death. In case of self-realization, one knows self, understands Him (inner energy) and get absolved of the cycle of action-reaction.

CHAPTER NINE

Inner Energy

Lord Krishna told that the supremacy of indestructible inner energy (God) is Ultimate truth and its eternal nature is embodied self and action abandoning source of desires and sentiments is desired action. Perishable nature of the objects is the basic principle of the phenomenal existence, and inner energy (soul) present in the body is its controller.

Understanding self means knowing inner energy. Understanding perishable nature of the objects including body, indestructible nature of inner energy and its being the controller is Ultimate truth.

The one who is able to remember Me at the time of the death achieves my gesture as one remembers that time what has been absorbed through continued contemplation. Therefore, remember Me all the time, and fight dedicating your mind and intelligence unto me. One contemplates Me in omniscient, controller, and tiny form yet controlling the universe, inconceivable sustainer of everything, and resplendent like sun.

At the semi-conscious or unconscious stage, one remembers what has been absorbed during most of the time in the mind. Similar to this, during death time, one remembers what has been absorbed during most of one's life through continued contemplation. Since, soul takes body immediately after leaving old body, one takes rebirth according to it. Therefore, one not only gets the result of lifetime performance but also carries over to the next birth. This realization may come only during death time if not realized earlier. Lord Krishna says that one should always continue to perform his dutiful action so that virtuousness is contemplated continuously.

Meditation is done withdrawing from the sense objects, with steady mind, deep inhaling and exhaling, chanting Om and concentrating into inner self. Living entities repeatedly take birth at the start of the Brahma's day and disappear at the beginning of night however inner energy situated within all living bodies does not perish.

Meditation is for concentration and control of the flickering mind hence done accordingly. There is a cycle of destruction and creation of a universe which is termed as night and day of Brahama. Even during destruction of the universe inner energy does not perish. From this inner energy, universe is recreated.

Persons with penance, involved in welfare, calm, having ultimate knowledge, self-realized and leaving this world during the six months of the sun in northward progression between winter solstice and summer solstice (*Uttarayan*) get *moksha* (liberation from the cycle of birth and death) while others are involved in the cycle of birth and death.

Penance is also the path to achieve self-realization. Penance can only be achieved with calmness, knowledge and continuous contemplation of virtuous actions during the lifetime.

Persons with penance, welfare, calmness, knowledge are self-realized. They remain happy and peaceful and do not get grieves. Those, such persons leaving this world during Uttarayan are full of inner and external energy as the weather and seasons are perfect and compound of happiness. Such a self-realized person, able to know self and inner energy gets liberated from the cycle of birth and death (attains moksha). When such souls do not take rebirth, their inner energy gets accumulated in Him. There is also a concept of taking rebirth by some of them along with Him to protect the universe.

Thus, it can be construed that all the souls take rebirth except those getting moksha (very few) and their number always remains constant. In case souls of humans are increasing, it is due to extinction of some other living entities or species. These living entities maybe living on ground, below ground, in water or air. As one living entity dies, it immediately takes birth in the form of same or some other species. The souls which get moksha generally do not take rebirth but are few and very rare.

CHAPTER TEN

External Energy

Lord Krishna said that I am pervaded in all the universes and supporting all living entities but I am not supported by them. I am the sustainer and protector of all living entities but never get attached to them or their nature. These creations enter into Me at the end of a fixed time cycle and I perform action and create them again and again in accordance to their nature and temperaments with My external energy source, remaining unattached to them though action is not binding on Me. All moving and non-moving entities are created from my external energy.

Supreme power supports all living entities of all the universes. That supreme power creates, sustains and destroys the creations. At the time of destruction of the universe, inner energy of all living entities enters into Him and then the universe is recreated at the end of a fixed cycle. Supreme power during the creation of the universe does not get attach to any of the creations either living or non-living. Thus, everyone gets the result of one's karma (actions), performed during this life and previous lives.

Persons of divine nature know and worship Me as immortal, of imperishable origin however ignorant consider Me in human and non-human forms. I am in everything including in non-living entities, knowledge, qualities, and cause and effects. I provide heat and rain, even hold it. I am immortality and death. Even those having faith in other deities, gain knowledge and get reward as per their source through Me but return to the world of mortals. Those believing in Me, meditating and devotedly following the path of attaining self-realization proceed towards Me.

Supreme power or inner energy is in everyone and everything including ideas, qualities, conditions, materials hence nothing is hidden from it. Therefore, one must remember that one's action (karma) is being watched and getting accounted by the supreme power. Those understanding it, remembering it and thus performing only virtuous action for the welfare of universe all the time as

God or supreme power does, proceed towards self-realization and moksha.

Followers and worshippers of deities, ancestors, ghosts, and spirits get along with their nature, go to them as per their worship and those worshipping Me come to Me. In the worship, I accept affectionately even a leaf, flower, fruit, water or action if devotedly offered to Me. So offer Me everything you perform and then you will be free from its auspicious or inauspicious reactions, and bondage of actions.

One's nature gets affected from those around, knowledge, ignorance and even to those worshipped or followed. One following to a particular person, gets influenced with his or her nature. Similarly, one worshipping to a particular deity gets influenced with the nature of the deity and one's nature changes accordingly. Those worshipping to spirits and ghosts also get influenced to their nature. Those worshipping to Him (God) get divine nature and engage themselves for the welfare of the universe. Hence, one must be careful in following or worshipping someone or selection of companion, partner, friend, guru, path or faith. He (God) becomes happy even with a flower, fruit, petal, water or simply by your action devotedly performed for the welfare of the universe however others may be wanting something in response of imparting knowledge, or discourse and even may not be satisfied with the offerings.

All living entities regardless of their birth in any section are equal to Me and neither are my friends nor foes but those offering themselves to Me are loved by Me. So, dedicate your body and mind unto Me considering it as your supreme goal.

He (God) neither differentiates among His creations nor gets attached to them. It is on the living entities to make a selection. If they love Him, He would love them however He never dislikes them due to equanimity. One gets result of one's actions (karma).

One moving on the path of self-realization, also does not differentiate between the creations and do not dislike them.

CHAPTER ELEVEN

Supreme Power

Lord Krishna told Arjun that neither deities nor great sages know My divine origin as I am the source of creation of deities and sages. The one who knows Me as never taken birth, having no origin, and the ultimate controller of all the universes, understands Me. All the diverse qualities like knowledge, wisdom, perception, compassion, truthfulness, control of senses and mind, pleasure, grief, fearlessness, austerity, charity, fame, infamy, contentment, equanimity, birth, death, and fear originate from Me alone. All seven great Sages and four Manus *(from whom universe is said to have been originated)* are originated from Me. I am the original cause of all causes and everything originates from Me. Those understanding that everything is from Me are knowledgeable.

There is a supreme power or destiny which creates universes, sustains and destroys them. Every creation of the universes is originated from Him. If one understands that every creation is from Him will respect others being a family member created from the very source, and as such becomes knowledgeable. On following it, one moves on the path of self-realization.

Some call Him God, some call Him Nature, some call him Guru, some destiny and some may call with different names and here we call Lord Krishna (Him).

Arjun asked, being unborn and supreme, only you personally know yourself so please describe the process of devotion to gain the Ultimate knowledge.

Lord Krishna told Arjun that I am in the soul of all living entities and their beginning, middle and the end. And I am in the sun, air, moon, knowledge, deities, *Rudra* (storm god), *yaksh* (demigods), *rakshas* (forest loving), *Kuber* (deity of wealth), fire, mountain, cobra, *Brahaspati* (guru), *Kartikey* (deity of landscape), ocean, *Bhrigu* (astrologer), sound, trees, sages, *gandharv* (messengers between deities and human), *yogi*, animals, kings, milk, weapons, water, *Yam* (deity of death), *Prahlad* (king of demons), time, lion, Garuda, wind, *Ram*, shark, river *Ganga*, knowledge, logics, letters, words, *Brahma*, fame, beauty, speech, memory, intellect, patience, compassion, month, season, *Gayatri mantra*, glory, victory, enterprise, nobility, *brahat sama*, gambling, *Vasudev, Arjun, Vyasdev, Sukracharya, daitya*, rod of punishment, strategy, silence, wisdom, and mind i.e. everywhere and in everything. I alone am the creator, sustainer, and destroyer of all the creations. I am also in the root cause of all living bodies. Thus, there is nothing which occurs or exists without Me. Everything including manifestations arise from a fraction of My glory and I support them from a fraction of My source.

Every creation said to be mortal or immortal, living or non-living, considered good or bad, small or big is from Him and as such nothing is to be hatred. In fact, it is He who supports and uses them for creation, sustaining and destruction of individuals and the universe from a fraction of His sources. Thus, one finds difficult to know the source of creation, sustaining and destruction. He is the doer but source maybe anyone and anything of the universe. And, He is not attached to anyone or anything hence one gets result of one's actions (karma).

CHAPTER TWELVE

Universal Form

Arjun then asked Lord Krishna to show His imperishable Ultimate form to him. Lord Krishna told Arjun that such form has not been seen even by those who can destroy living entities in no time as whole universe of moving and stationary celestial bodies are situated in only a tiny part of the Ultimate form and your present eyes will not be able to see it so I grant you the divine sight.

Though, everyone might be interested to see God but always want to see in the form of creator or sustainer and not in the form of death though God is creator, sustainer and destroyer. Lord Krishna showed Arjun all the three forms in a single form by providing him the divine sight.

Lord Krishna showed him the Ultimate form which had innumerable heads, faces, mouths, eyes, and arms in all the directions. Arjun saw divine attires and ornaments worn by Him, armed with innumerable rare weapons. Then he saw thousands of suns simultaneously blazing around Him, complete universe situated in Him at a small place along with all species of the living entities, sages, deities, having no beginning, middle and end.

God has different heads, different faces, mouths, eyes and arms in all the directions. Therefore, one has to realize that God sees everything. Also, He may create, sustain and destruct from any form, any direction and any source though Arjun saw so far only creation and sustaining forms.

Then Arjun saw blazing fire from few of His mouths like sun radiating scorching heat making very difficult to look towards them. Arjun saw living entities being supported by Him, and also being destroyed by Him. He saw His infinite energy, fierce eyes like sun and cool like moon, blazing fire in His mouths with living bodies going into them, deities and deities praying, beautiful and also dreadful teeth, i.e. Ultimate form having kind, and deathly faces so also performing actions accordingly. The Ultimate form was clearly showing creation, sustaining and destruction of the universes inside Him simultaneously all universes including deities, and demi Gods situated in Him. Arjun understood that everything is situated in God and is from Him. He is the creator, sustainer and destructor.

Here Arjun could see all three forms of God i.e. creator, sustainer and destroyer.

Then Arjun saw one of fiery mouth in which all his kin, relatives, friends, kings and soldiers standing before him in the battlefield were entering and perishing. Thereafter, he started trembling looking to death God in Him and asked Him to reveal His identity. Lord Krishna told that those whom he was seeing as perishing were actually going to die soon whether he fights or doesn't. Therefore, you be a medium and conquer the enemy including Dronacharya, Bhishm, Jaydrath, Karn as their death has already been assigned by Him.

Arjun could see death form of God destroying even to those whom he respected and loved or was supposed to fight. Thus, it is the God doing everything through His creations. And one has to perform always virtuous action for the self-benefit.

One has to remember that death is not even predictable by knowledgeable as Arjun could see Bhishm and Dronacharya entering into the mouth of death God. As such, death may come any time hence one should not postpone virtuous action for the future rather perform continuously. when one realizes it, moves on the path of self-realization.

Arjun then prayed to Him and told Lord that though he considered Him his friend, has now understood His identity. He is everything in the universe and there was nothing equal to Him so requested Him to come in his former form. Lord Krishna told Arjun that only he has seen His Ultimate form and no one else and then came in Lord *Vishnu* form for a moment thereafter in normal two armed Krishna's form.

Seeing death is always painful, particularly of near and dear ones. Only a person moving on the path of self-realization is able to move away from its feeling.

CHAPTER THIRTEEN

Devotion

Arjun wanted to know whether only devotees worshipping Him in perceptible form are able to gain Ultimate knowledge or those worshipping in non-perceptible form can also get it. Lord told Arjun that irrespective of the form worshipped, it is the dedication in Me that enables one to know Me however those having equanimity to every situation and to everything, and dedicated to the welfare of all living entities understands Me and are able to achieve Me. Success to those worshipping in non-perceptible form is achieved with great difficulty but those worshipping Me with complete dedication, attachment and offering all activities unto Me, gains Ultimate knowledge as I also help them.

One worships God or supreme power in perceptible or non-perceptible form. One can reach the state of self-realization by following both the paths. However, when one sees something or someone, following becomes easy. Therefore, flowing in perceptible form becomes easy for a devotee. But, one can know God with both the forms of devotion provided worshipping is with dedication.

Worship should lead to the path of performing virtuous action for the welfare of others without any desire or getting attached to its result. Those seeking self-realization and worshipping Him with dedication, attachment and offering all actions to Him for the welfare of the universe are also helped by Him.

For the dedication, one has to practice and meditate. If the one is not able to achieve Ultimate knowledge, moves ahead towards the goal. In case, one is unable to concentrate in Me, should perform action without attachment to the desire of its result.

One must realize that dedication comes from the practice and meditation. Practice and meditation never go waste as one moves towards dedication even if not completely successful.

Knowledge is better than self-experience, meditation is considered superior to only knowledge, and performing virtuous action without desire of the result of action is even better than the meditation. Understanding of this leads to tranquility and ultimate knowledge.

Knowledge is better than gaining self-experience as it avoids pain and saves time to achieve the goal. Knowledge with meditation is still better than only knowledge. And performing virtuous action without desire of its result is still better. Thus, a combination of knowledge, meditation and performing virtuous action leads to self-realization.

The devotee who is non-envious to all living entities, having no attachment to the possessions, away from ego, having equanimity during pleasure and grief, contended, forgiving, able to control self, determined, dedicated and knowledgeable is always dear to Me. Such a person is never disturbed from anyone and no one feels disturbed from him. He remains undisturbed from pleasure, anger, fear and grief. Unattached to material desires, he is kind, knowledgeable, undisturbed, worriless, performing action and taking all situations with ease, thus, having equanimity to both favourable and unfavorable situations. Such a person treats enemy and friend, honour and dishonor, cold and heat, pleasure and grief, praise and criticism equally, and is free from attachment to the material world, remaining contented with and what comes on its accord.

A self-realized person is kind, knowledgeable, undisturbed, worriless, performing action, treating enemy and friend, honour and dishonor, cold and heat, pleasure and grief, praise and criticism equally, free from attachment to material world, remaining contented with and what comes on its accord taking all situations with ease having equanimity under all situations. Person having such traits is said to have reached the state of self-realization and remains happy and peaceful.

Even if one is not able to reach the state of self-realization, moving towards its path is helpful to attain peace.

CHAPTER FOURTEEN

Source and Domain

Arjun then asked Lord to explain the source, the domain of activities, the knower of the domain, knowledge and the purpose of the knowledge. Lord told Arjun that the body is the domain of activities, and the one who knows it, is the knower of the domain. Those who know Me (Inner energy) being within all bodies is the knower of the knowledge. Ego, wisdom, unknown nature of material desires, ten senses (eyes, ears, nose, tongue, hands, feet, mouth, skin, ling and anus) along with mind, five objects of the senses as hearing, seeing, taste, touch, and smell, desire, consciousness, grief, pleasure, malice, determination, all combined are the field of activities modified by the transformation carried out in the body to understand life cycle beginning with birth and ending with death through humility, kindness, non-violence, tolerance, honesty, charity, cleanliness, steadfastness, self-control, senses control, self-realization, equanimity, welfare service, and Ultimate knowledge for realizing the Ultimate truth.

All the actions are performed by the body and for the body hence body is the domain of activities. Mind is also part of the body. In the body, field of activities like ego, wisdom, manifestation towards desires, senses along with mind, objects of the senses, desire, consciousness, grief, pleasure, malice, determination, individually or combined are carried out for the self-body or other's. One having knowledge to perform the type of activities and its purpose is the knower. Activities performed through humility, kindness, non-violence, tolerance, honesty, charity, cleanliness, steadfastness, self-control, senses control, following equanimity under all situations, with service for welfare, attaining self-realization is the ultimate purpose of life and its knowhow is the knowledge. One knowing it is the knower.

Now, I will explain about what is to be known for the truth. It is to be known that with hands, eyes, heads, and faces, He is everywhere, seeing everything, hearing everything, and existing in everything. The truth is that

He is the knower of all the senses still remains unattached to them, sustainer to everything still unattached to them, and maintainer of everything including materialism still not involved in it. He is within all living entities still living away from them, stationary but mobile at all the time, of subatomic size still incomprehensible, very far still too near, non-divisible still divided among various living entities, creator and sustainer of all living entities also the destroyer, illuminator of all that illuminates beyond the darkness of the knowledge. One should understand the field of activities, knower of the activities and knowledge to understand Me.

Ultimate truth is that He is everywhere and in everything, always seeing and hearing everything hence nothing can go unnoticed from Him. One understanding and following it, will never harm anyone, always respect others and will do no wrongdoing to individuals and the universe thus reaching to the stage of self-realization.

Energy and knowledge are beginning less and transformation of the body and three temperaments are produced by this material energy as the energy is responsible for the cause and effect action for experiencing pleasure and grief and inner energy experiences three temperaments, as He is within the body, supreme to the individual consciousness, preserver, happiness provider, and ultimate controller. Anyone having knowledge of inner energy, individual consciousness, three temperaments and Ultimate knowledge is knowledgeable. Some seek the knowledge within the Self by meditating on Self and others unite individual consciousness with the Ultimate knowledge differentiating between self and inner energy. Yet others having heard from others engage themselves in worship. Whatever living entities know, anyone perceiving Me in all living entities, everywhere as imperishable within the perishable, has actual perception of Ultimate knowledge. By perceiving so, one doesn't degrade embodied Self and anyone perceiving so considers self is non doer and performs action as being performed only by Me and the life cycle is from the inner energy.

Energy is responsible for cause and effect action. One according to external energy will have temperaments. Inner energy experiences the temperaments and depending on inner energy one seeks knowledge of Self. If one depends upon external or material energy, its effect would come into him or her cause being external energy similarly one depending upon inner energy gets its effect.

One has many ways to understand Me like knowledge, worship, meditation on self. But, one perceiving Me in all living entities, situated everywhere, and imperishable even after living in perishable has the ultimate knowledge. Thus,

He is in all entities whether perishable or imperishable however perishable objects and bodies get destroyed but not He or inner energy.

CHAPTER FIFTEEN

Temperaments

Divine nature is neither reborn during universal creation nor destroyed during universal destruction. Entire material energy is through womb of all species and thus temperaments (गुण) produced from the material energy are inherited by birth in all living entities. Three temperaments *Satgun* (verity), *Rajogun* (extravagance) and *Tamogun* (vileness) take control of individual's consciousness and enslave Self within the body. Among these three, verity being pious and enlightening, leads to happiness and wisdom, extravagance to the possessions, lust, greed, attachment and strong material desires, and vileness to addiction, inadvertency, laziness, infatuation and anger. Any temperament can overpower the other two i.e. verity can overpower extravagance and vileness, extravagance to verity and vileness, and vileness to verity and extravagance.

Divine nature comes from inner energy hence is indestructible. External or material energy produces temperaments i.e. Satogun or Satgun (temperament of verity), Rajogun (temperament of extravagance) and Tamogun (temperament of vileness). Satogun is the temperament inducing action for truth, knowledge, other's welfare and self-realization. Rajogun is the temperament tempting action for possessions, greed, lust, attachments, power and ego. Tamogun induces addiction, laziness, infatuation, anger, and inadvertency. Everyone has all the three temperaments and any temperament can overpower other two anytime in case of uncontrolled mind. However, one moving on the path of self-realization has predominant verity temperament.

When knowledge is produced, verity predominates. When greed, lust and desires for sense gratification arise, extravagance predominates and when inertness, neglect and illusion arise, vileness predominates. From verity, wisdom gets developed, from extravagance, greed and from vileness, inebriation.

One has all the three temperaments produced from the material energy. Therefore, a person shows nature as per the prevailing temperament. Same person may have all three temperaments in a day and even within a gap of a short period. Therefore, one's behavior and action would vary according to the prevailing temperament at a particular time. Since, these are from external energy, uncontrolled mind can lead to switching over from a particular temperament to other in no time. A self-realized person has control over the mind and performs only virtuous action due to verity temperament.

After death one with verity temperament takes birth to those engaged in knowledge, with extravagance temperament to those attached to material desires, and with vileness temperament in animal species.

Effect of temperaments continues during rebirth and a person of predominant temperament shows the symptoms of pervious birth. A new born child brings temperament from the previous birth.

Action with verity temperament leads to righteous result, with extravagance to stress and with vileness to stupidity.

Any action carried out with verity temperament will lead to contentment, carried out with extravagance to stress and with vileness to stupidity.

Verity develops wisdom, extravagance greed and vileness inadvertence and attachment. Those with verity temperament go to higher level, with extravagance to midlevel and with vileness to hellish situation.

Temperaments enhance or reduce the wisdom. Verity opens up inner energy and cover up external energy while extravagance and vileness hide it and open external or material energy. Verity temperament leads one towards self-realization due to wisdom and knowledge.

When one understands that all the actions are evolved only from these three temperaments and performs action according to *Satgun* (verity), achieves divine nature. Those rising beyond the three temperaments achieve immortality thus leaving birth, death, old age, and misery of material world and treat pleasure & grief, soil, stone & gold, honour & insult, friends & enemies equally qualifying for renunciation and inaction in action. One who attains such knowledge and unites it with the devotion, qualifies for self-realization.

One takes up activities according to one's temperament at a particular time. Once a particular temperament overpowers other two, it may take control of mind and senses. Therefore, for moving on the path of self-realization, one has to practice and follow verity temperament through knowledge, devotion, worship, meditation, renunciation, and performing virtuous action (karma).

CHAPTER SIXTEEN

Self-realization

Lord Krishna told that concept of self-realization can be understood from an inverted Banyan tree having large number of branches and leaves below and roots above, branches symbolizing to sense objects developed due to temperaments and roots spreading downward symbolizing actions and reactions produced from the senses.

Concept of self-realization can be understood from an inverted Banyan tree which has too many branches and leaves at bottom and stem towards top including many secondary roots. This is somewhat like a triangle with many lines connecting base to the vertex. To attain state of self-realization, one has to reach at top. However, senses representing branches stops one to reach at the top i.e. to attain the state of self-realization.

It is difficult to perceive an inverted tree, its beginning and main root without understanding the effect of material desires and attachment for self-realization. Knowledgeable attain it by practicing virtuousness continuously through embodied inner energy, giving up attachment, evils, lust, and dualities through body and mind as the effect of the material energy is carried out by mind and six senses. Attaining self-realization, one does not return back and enlightens the world like sun, moon, and fire, illuminating for others.

One has to have knowledge to reach the state of self-realization which can only be attained by practicing virtuousness continuously through inner energy simultaneously giving up effects of material energy i.e. possessions, greed, lust, attachments, power, ego, addiction, laziness, infatuation, anger, and inadvertency.

Inner energy enters into a new body from the departed body, carries knowledge and temperaments governing sense objects i.e. hearing, seeing, taste, touch, smell and mind. Knowledgeable understands the inner energy departing from the body and transferred into new body, residing in the body and enjoying the body however others get mesmerized and are unable to perceive its potency. Remember, even sun, moon, fire, plants, and all living entities get energy from the potency of inner energy. Energy in living bodies is provided for digestion of all four types of foods i.e. eaten, sucked, drunk or licked.

One is not able to perceive unlimited potency of inner energy as gets mesmerized from external energy. Unaware of the potency of inner energy or unable to perceive it, people do not attempt the path of self-realization or leave it after moving on it for some time.

There are only two known principles in fourteen universal systems of three worlds as perishable and imperishable. All moving and stationary living bodies are perishable and inner energy (God) imperishable. Controller is someone else who is imperishable and sustainer of everything and anyone. One who understands it, attains self-realization.

One should understand that inner energy has unlimited potency and is imperishable and He is the controller of all the universes, both of perishable and imperishable bodies but Himself as imperishable. One who understands it and has its knowledge, moves towards attaining self-realization.

CHAPTER SEVENTEEN

Divine and Demonic Paths

Lord Krishna told Arjun about two types of nature as divine and demonic. Fearlessness, pure heart, knowledge, kindness, self-control, renunciation, austerity, uprightness, humbleness, nonviolence, truthfulness, aversion of fault finding, forgiveness, purity, benevolence, compassion, generousness, gentleness, modesty, determination, gracefulness, and courage are in the divine nature. Hypocrisy, egoism, conceit, anger, harshness and ignorance are part of demonic nature. Divine nature liberates material desires while demonic nature causes attachment to material desires. Those having demonic nature are not able to understand even best and worst actions due to their bad conduct, and absence of verity. In absence of the Ultimate knowledge and ignorance of the soul (inner energy), persons with demonic nature get engaged in violent activities detrimental to the universe.

There are two types of nature as divine and demonic. Divine nature ultimately leads to liberation of material desires and demonic nature attachment to them. One with divine nature can only attain self-realization as it is for the welfare of the universe while demonic nature is for detrimental activities.

Those with demonic nature consider universe without creator, supreme controller, without cause, originating from lust. Addicted to insatiable lust, arrogance, ego and illusion, demonic engage themselves in devilish activities. Those of demonic nature consider gratification of senses as the highest goal of the life, entangling into lust, arrogance, power, and ego, leading to envious, cruel, evil and harmful nature. I have gained it today, I will have it tomorrow, I have killed him, I will kill him tomorrow, I am the controller, I am enjoying, I am powerful, I am rich, I am aristocratic, I am perfect, I will sacrifice, I will give in charity, and I am superior to others; are part of demonic nature due to ignorance as demonic nature leads to falsehood assuming the universe without creator and controller, living the life of illusions, fear, anxieties and anger.

Demonic nature takes one towards egotism, sense gratifications, temperaments of extravagance and vileness, and away from the path of self-realization.

Demonic nature has envious and blaspheme feeling living in the world of illusions and innumerable fears, anxieties, anger, greed, material desires, detrimental to soul searching and attaining the path of self-realization, and persons with such nature take rebirth with same nature. Arjun, one should leave lust, anger and greed being detrimental to self-realization.

Demonic nature is detrimental to self-realization while divine nature leads one towards it. Since nature is also carried over during rebirth, persons with demonic nature continue detrimental activities during their next birth.

One who does not follow divine nature under the impulse of desires, never reaches to self-realization, attains happiness and goal of life.

One not following divine nature i.e. not performing action for the welfare of the others never reaches to self-realization, happiness and peace.

CHAPTER EIGHTEEN

Threefold Path

Lord Krishna told that one gets the temperament as per the nature of previous life and the faith comes as per the perception of mind. Those of verity temperament worship Me (God), of extravagance to demigods (*yaksh who are said to be the guards of treasure*) and of vileness to spirits and ghosts.

Temperaments affect the nature during rebirth while mind the faith. Normally, mind controls the temperaments but when a particular temperament becomes strong, it may take over control of the mind.

One worships and has faith on those who are according to one's temperament. Since verity temperament is related to virtuous action, it inspires one to worship God or follow to virtuousness. Those with extravagance temperament, get inspired with deities or demigods or gurus known to fulfil the desires of possessions, greed, lust, attachments, ego and power and of vileness temperament worship to spirits and ghosts being desirous of addiction, laziness, infatuation, anger, and inadvertency. Similarly, one follows others or becomes friendly to those having same temperament. As temperaments change from time to time, one also switches over to worshipping or following others from time to time according to the prevailing temperament at that particular time.

Those not having mankind knowledge, indiscriminately exploit the five elements comprising the body – earth, water, fire, air and space out of pride, ego, and material desires. There are three kinds of food, sacrifices, austerities and charity. Foods promoting life, vitality, health, happiness and contentment are liked by those having verity temperament, very bitter, salty, sour, hot, dry, pungent, burning foods by those of extravagance temperament and semi cooked, left over, impure foods and having lost its original state, taste, and essence are liked by those having vileness temperament.

Temperaments are very forceful and one carries various activities according to them. Even five elements of the body which are lifeline of the living bodies are exploited indiscriminately by those having extravagance and vileness temperaments due pride, ego, material desires and ignorance.

Food habits are also related to the temperament. Pious foods are eaten by those having verity temperament which are good for life, vitality, health, happiness and contentment hence leading to self-realization. Foods which are bitter, salty, sour, dry, pungent, burning are related to the temperament of extravagance while half cooked, left over, impure, and stale foods to the temperament of vileness. Thus, for self-realization one has to eat pious and pure foods.

Sacrifice without desires and performed as one's duty is in the nature of verity, with desires and for self-benefit of extravagance and performed without charity and faith, and carried out inappropriately belongs to vileness.

Sacrifice has to be made without desires and attachment to the desire of its result. Those having verity temperament make sacrifice accordingly while those having extravagance temperament for self-benefit due to greed and ego. Those with vileness temperament due to ignorance may make sacrifice inappropriately. Thus, sacrifice without any desire and made appropriately only leads to self-realization.

Austerity of the body is the worship of God and wise gurus (teachers) with engagement in the welfare of living entities, cleanliness, simplicity, celibacy and non-violence towards living entities. Austerity of speech is serenity, pleasing, beneficial and inoffensive to others. Austerity of mind is serenity of thoughts, pleasing, peaceful, self-controlled and welfare to others. Those with verity temperament practice austerities without desires, of extravagance temperament for gaining popularity, respect, adoration and money and of vileness for causing harm and pain to others and even to self.

For self-realization, austerity is also important. Austerity is also related to the temperaments. Austerity has to be in the body, speech, and mind. Those with verity temperament practice austerity for the welfare of other and without any desire while with extravagance temperament practice it for gratification of their desires and of vileness temperament to cause harm and give pain to others or even to self. To move on self-realization path, one has to adopt austerity with verity temperament.

Charity without any consideration at a sanctified place, given as a matter of duty to a qualifying person is in the nature of verity, given with the expectation of some return, desire or compulsion is in the nature of extravagance and given disrespectfully, unceremoniously at an inappropriate time and place is in the nature of vileness.

Temperaments also affect the charity, its giver and receiver, time of its giving and place of giving. To move on the path of self-realization, the charity has to be for the welfare of others, to a qualifying person, given respectfully at appropriate time and place. The charity for self-benefit with desire of some return or compulsion due to extravagance temperament and given disrespectfully at inappropriate time and place due to vileness temperament does not lead to self-realization. Thus, for self-realization, one has to adopt verity temperament and give charity.

Factual, true and universal sound (Om Tat Sat) indicating significance of Ultimate truth is performed promising sacrifice, charity and austerity for the welfare of the Universe.

And one must remember that there is a supreme power which controls everything and thus to realize it one has to move on the path of self-realization by performing sacrifice, charity and austerity for the welfare of the universe.

CHAPTER NINETEEN

Sacrifice

Lord Krishna then told about sacrifice or renunciation. Some say abandonment of activities linked with material desires is renunciation and some say giving up the desires of results of all actions is renunciation but some feel actions performed for sacrifice, charity and austerity should not be renounced. Lord Krishna told that actions performed for sacrifice, charity and austerity should never be renounced as they purify even to learned and should be performed as duty.

Sacrifice, austerity and charity are essential part of self-realization however in every case, one has to perform action. Hence, performing action is essential part of self-realization.

Lord Krishna told that renouncing action altogether is the temperament of vileness and renunciation out of fear of body discomfort or misery is the temperament of extravagance. Arjun, giving up desire of result of performing action of specified duty is renunciation and of verity temperament. Living entities never give up action completely.

Renouncing action altogether is not renunciation so also performing action for body comfort or to avoid fear of misery. Thus, temperaments are also related to renunciation. Verity temperament inspires one to renounce material desires, extravagance to renounce those actions leading to discomfort and misery and vileness to renounce actions themselves. Renunciation of material desires without leaving performing action (karma) leads to the path of self-realization.

Cause of all proper or improper actions performed by body, speech and mind are power, ego, senses, trying something different, and knowledge. Knowledge, the goal of the knowledge and the knower of the knowledge become the impetus of action based on total of the endeavour, performed action and the doer, according to the temperament. The knowledge by which one sees all the living entities without division is of verity, seeing diversity within living entities of extravagance and with fragmental conception the nature of vileness.

All activities are taken up for sense gratifications (body needs), power, ego, innovation, knowledge and self-realization. One performs action based on the knowledge, goal of the knowledge, and efforts enable to put in. Thus, the result of the action is according to the sum total of knowledge, goal of the knowledge, and efforts put therein.

With the knowledge, one knows about the action to be performed as knowledge by which one sees everyone without division is of verity temperament. Such a person moves towards self-realization and those seeing everyone with diversity, or with fragmental concept do not attain self-realization due to extravagance and vileness temperaments and their inadequate knowledge or ignorance.

The action performed without any material desires, free from attachment and arrogance and performed as duty is of verity temperament. The action with material desires or ego satisfaction is of extravagance and the action performed out of illusion without considering consequences, and one's capability is of vileness temperament.

When one has verity temperament is calm and peaceful hence performs action (karma) for other's welfare without anger. During extravagance temperament, one performs action for self-benefit and ego satisfaction and during vileness temperament action is performed for illusion or fantasy. Therefore, calmness and peace are essential to attain self-realization as a self-realized person does not have anger, ego and material desires and does not live in dreams or fantasies.

The action performer performing egoless action, with great enthusiasm, unaffected by its success and failure has the temperament of verity, performing action with desires affected by greed, its success or failure leading to joy or grief is of extravagance while performing action deceptively with laziness and depression is of vileness temperament.

Verity temperament leads to performing egoless action with great enthusiasm, and equanimity from its success and failure while extravagance to performing action for greed and vileness to performing deceptive action. Thus, a person moving on the path of self-realization performs egoless action with great enthusiasm.

Arjun, the nature of verity leads to the Ultimate knowledge, the nature of extravagance to imperfect knowledge and of vileness temperament to ignorance.

One having verity temperament gains knowledge of self-realization, having extravagance temperament imperfect knowledge and having vileness temperament no knowledge of self-realization.

The nature of verity temperament has uninterrupted determination motivating the action to attain the Ultimate knowledge, extravagance of getting desires of senses fulfilled motivated by the result, and vileness of fear and depression without any motivation.

Motivation during verity temperament is attainment of knowledge and self-realization, motivation during extravagance temperament is sense gratification while there is no motivation during vileness temperament.

The happiness arising from the serenity of the Ultimate knowledge or self-realization is in the nature of verity temperament leading to contentment and peace in the end though bitter at the beginning. The pleasure and ego satisfaction arising from the fulfillment of desires of the senses and possessions is in the nature of extravagance temperament leading to bitterness or stress at the end though momentous joy in the beginning. Pleasure arising without performing action, misleading to self is of the nature of vileness temperament.

Verity temperament leads to self-contentment and happiness due to self-realization though path of self-realization is bitter at the beginning. Extravagance temperament provides momentary pleasure and ego satisfaction at the beginning but becomes bitter at the end. Vileness temperament leads to momentary pleasure due to fantasies but anger and depression at the end.

Everyone in the universe is influenced from the three modes of the temperaments. The activities of *brahman, kshatriya, vaishya* and *shudra* are divided according to the temperaments. The *brahman* have the qualities of serenity, self-control, austerity, purity, tolerance, honesty, knowledge, wisdom and faith, the *kshatriya* of brevity, exuberance, determination, resourcefulness, courage, generosity and leadership, *vaishya* of agriculture and trade and *shudra* of services. One performs action and achieves perfection according to one's qualification. Though one has to perform one's action perfectly, performing own action imperfectly is better than doing other's action perfectly hence one should select his duty accordingly to one's nature. One gets perfection by performing it without attachment to material desires, controlling the mind.

Those having serenity, self-control, austerity, purity, tolerance, honesty, knowledge, wisdom and faith are said to be brahman, having brevity, exuberance, determination, resourcefulness, courage, generosity and leadership are said to be kshatriya, having trade and agriculture are said to be vaishya and engaged in services as shudra. Everyone is influenced from three temperaments. Thus, one may perform action of brahman, kshatriya, vaishya or shudra according to the prevailing temperament.

One should perform one's action perfectly else practice for it. It is better to perform own duty imperfectly and practice for its perfection before taking up other's duty with or without perfection. Thus, one should look for perfecting one's duty first.

Arjun, one gets qualified to attain the Ultimate knowledge on getting fully purified, self-controlled, giving up desires for sense gratification, avoiding materialistic company (persons), moderate in eating, keeping control on body, mind and speech, absorbed in yoga, unattached to senses, having no ego, pride, anger and material desires, generous, peaceful, self-contented, having equanimity to all living bodies and in all situations, and always conscious to Me. Another way is to surrender yourself to me completely.

One reaches towards the state of self-realization when fully purified, self-controlled, having given up material desires for sense gratification, avoiding materialistic company (persons), moderate in eating, keeping control on body, mind and speech, absorbed in yoga, unattached to senses, having no ego, pride, anger and material desires, generous, calm and peaceful, self-contented, having equanimity to all living bodies and in all situations, and devoted to Him. Thus, attaining the stage of self-realization is not easy and is very difficult.

Another way to self-realization is to surrender to Him completely from the body and mind i.e. perform action for the welfare of others though body and mind as He does.

And then Arjun with stable mind became ready to fight.

CHAPTER TWENTY

Understanding Self-realization

Let us discuss self-realization from the Chapter 15 in which concept of self-realization was related to an inverted Banyan tree having many branches and leaves at bottom and stem towards the top including many secondary roots as shown in Figure 1.

Figure 1: Inverted Banyan Tree

This is somewhat like a triangle tmarked as ABC with many lines connecting base to the vertex (Figure 2). For reaching self-realization stage one has to reach at the top of the triangle i.e. vertex A.

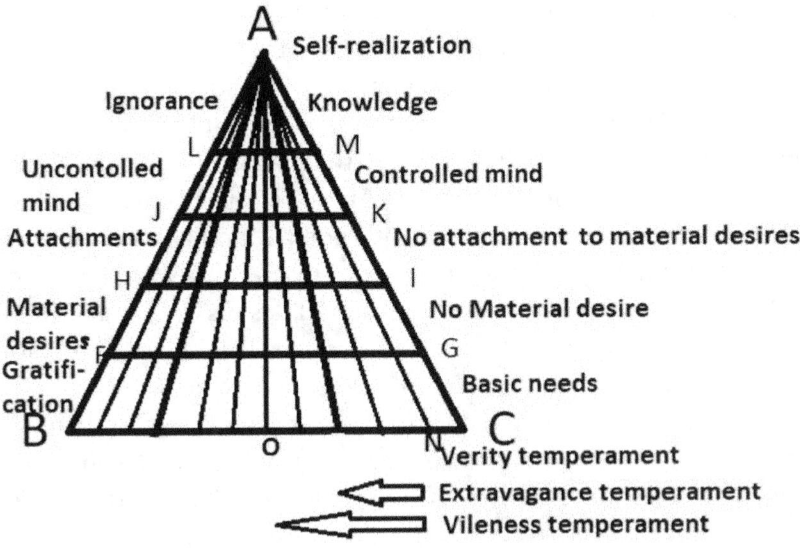

Figure 2: Triangle of Self-realization

The banyan tree has large number of branches and leaves, branches symbolizing to sense objects developed due to the temperaments and roots spreading downward symbolizing actions and reactions produced from the senses. These are being represented by the lines drawn from vertex A to the base BC representing sense objects gratifying body needs, desires, attachments, mind control and knowledge of self-realization. These sense objects are developed due to the temperaments.

Above concept is being tried to be represented in the form of a triangle ABC. Six levels are assumed in the triangle as given in the following;

1. Body needs
2. Material desires
3. Attachment to material desires
4. Control of mind
5. Ultimate knowledge
6. Self-realization

From Figure 2, the following inferences may be drawn;

1. To attain ultimate knowledge, one has to control mind, pass through attachments, material desires and needs before reaching to the state of self-realization. One cannot reach to self-realization state surpassing needs, material desires, attachments, mind control and knowledge.
2. Point C in the triangle is considered as the starting point to move.
3. One may move up theoretically from C to the path G, I, K, M, and A but it is not practically feasible as one has to fulfill basic needs to survival.
4. Therefore, a triangle will be formed with point C on base and another point say N on the base with A as vertex to reach self-realization state. This triangle will have few needs, few material desires, few attachment, little uncontrolled mind and considerable knowledge. Still this path would be the shortest path to reach self-realization point A.
5. If one is attracted to higher order of needs, higher order of material desires, and higher order of attachments, it would lead to more and more uncontrolled mind and lesser knowledge and the length of path to reach self-realization would go on increasing. In such case, it would be difficult for one to attain self-realization state as the life span is limited until suddenly someone moves towards right side on higher level surrendering desires, attachments with control of mind.
6. With more and more needs, material desires and attachments, less control of mind, less knowledge, the temperaments of extravagance and vileness will force one to move more and more towards left making path of self-realization longer and longer. Hence, it would be more and more difficult to attain self-realization.
7. However, from any point on any level with verity temperament, one can climb up by moving towards right path surrendering needs, material desires, attachments, with more control of mind and more knowledge however extravagance or vileness temperaments if predominant will force one to move further towards right making the path further longer.
8. Since, the extravagance and vileness temperaments forces one away from right to left side i.e. towards higher order of needs, material desires, attachments leading to uncontrolled mind and lesser knowledge, one is not able to reach self-realization state.

Inspiration From Bhagwadgita

Bhagwadgita inspires to;

1. Exercise control (control of desires, attachments and mind) for self-contentment
2. Remain calm to practice verity temperament (keep away from anger, do meditation, perform action like inaction, engage yourself in charity, devotion, sacrifice, and worship)
3. Practice to move away from grieves (even from the grief of death of a near and dear one)
4. Practice self-contentment to remain happy (Perform your duty and leave result on Supreme power)
5. Perform virtuous action dedicatedly with a goal to do it perfectly
6. Make a goal to achieve self-realization
7. Attain peace